Busy Ant Maths

2ND EDITION

Textbook 2

T0321867

Series editor and author: Peter Clarke

William Collins' dream of knowledge for all began with the publication of his first book in 1819.

A self-educated mill worker, he not only enriched millions of lives, but also founded a flourishing publishing house. Today, staying true to this spirit, Collins books are packed with inspiration, innovation and practical expertise.

They place you at the centre of a world of possibility and give you exactly what you need to explore it.

Collins. Freedom to teach.

Published by Collins

An imprint of HarperCollins*Publishers*
The News Building, 1 London Bridge Street, London, SE1 9GF, UK

HarperCollins*Publishers*
Macken House, 39/40 Mayor Street Upper, Dublin 1, D01 C9W8, Ireland

Browse the complete Collins catalogue at
collins.co.uk

10 9 8 7 6 5 4 3 2 1

ISBN 978-0-00-861373-0

British Library Cataloguing-in-Publication Data

A catalogue record for this publication is available from the British Library.

Series editor: Peter Clarke
Author: Peter Clarke
Product manager: Holly Woolnough
Editorial assistant: Nalisha Vansia
Copy editor: Tanya Solomons
Proofreader: Catherine Dakin
Illustrator: Ann Paganuzzi
Cover designer: Amparo Barrera
Cover illustrator: Amparo Barrera
Internal designer: 2Hoots Publishing Services
Typesetter: David Jimenez
Production controller: Alhady Ali
Printed and bound in Great Britain by Martins the Printers

Busy Ant Maths 2nd edition components are compatible with the 1st edition of Busy Ant Maths.

This book is produced from independently certified FSC™ paper to ensure responsible forest management.

For more information visit: harpercollins.co.uk/green

Acknowledgements

p44t BlueRingMedia/Shutterstock; p45t VikiVector/ Shutterstock; p45b Nikiteev_konstantin/Shutterstock; p52–53 Zern Liew/Shutterstock; p54tc Creativika Graphics/ Shutterstock; p56tc Rosemary Calvert/Getty Images; p57c StockAppeal/Shutterstock; p58ctl Dream01/Shutterstock; p58bcl Creativika Graphics/Shutterstock; p59cr Net Vector/ Shutterstock.

Contents

Multiplication and division

Fractions

Year 2 Number Facts

How to use this book

This book shows different pictures, models and images (representations) to explain important mathematical ideas to do with number.

The key words related to the mathematical ideas are shown in **colour**. It's important that you understand what each of these words mean.

At the start of each double page is a brief description of the key mathematical ideas.

The main part of each double page explains the mathematical ideas. It might include pictures, models or an example.

Your teacher will talk to you about the images on the pages.

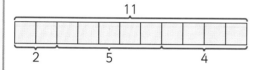

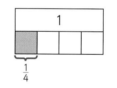

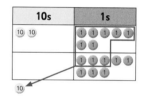

Sometimes there might be questions to think about or an activity to do.

Pages 6–7

This refers to mathematical ideas on other pages that you need to understand before learning about the ideas on these two pages.

Pages 10–11, 14–17, 20–43

This refers to mathematical ideas on other pages that use or build upon the ideas on these two pages.

 This helps you think more deeply about the mathematical ideas.

 Use the pages in this book to help you answer the questions in the Activity Books.

Read, write and count numbers to 100

In all areas of maths, it is important to be able to count objects to 100 and represent these in both numerals and words.

> You should be able to read and write numbers to 10.

> The numbers from 11 to 19 – the **teen numbers** – can be tricky.

0 1 2 3 4 5 6 7 8 9 10 11 12 13 14 15 16 17 18 19 20

11
1 **ten** and 1 **one**
eleven

12
1 **ten** and 2 **ones**
twelve

13
1 **ten** and 3 **ones**
thirteen

14
1 **ten** and 4 **ones**
fourteen

15
1 **ten** and 5 **ones**
fifteen

16
1 **ten** and 6 **ones**
sixteen

17
1 **ten** and 7 **ones**
seventeen

18
1 **ten** and 8 **ones**
eighteen

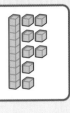

19
1 **ten** and 9 **ones**
nineteen

What numbers are shown below?

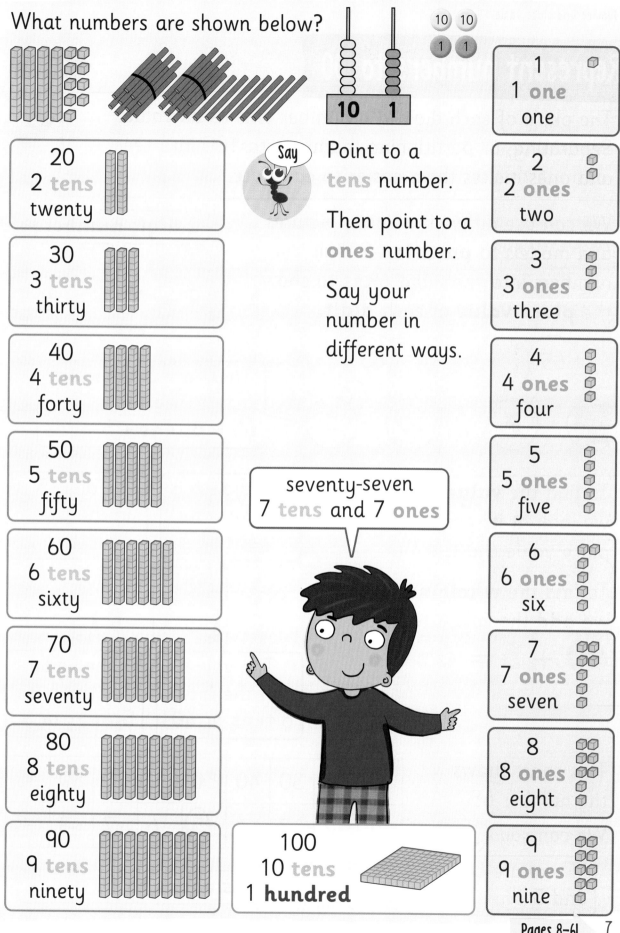

Say Point to a **tens** number.

Then point to a **ones** number.

Say your number in different ways.

seventy-seven
7 **tens** and 7 **ones**

20	2 **tens**	twenty
30	3 **tens**	thirty
40	4 **tens**	forty
50	5 **tens**	fifty
60	6 **tens**	sixty
70	7 **tens**	seventy
80	8 **tens**	eighty
90	9 **tens**	ninety

100
10 **tens**
1 **hundred**

1	1 **one**	one
2	2 **ones**	two
3	3 **ones**	three
4	4 **ones**	four
5	5 **ones**	five
6	6 **ones**	six
7	7 **ones**	seven
8	8 **ones**	eight
9	9 **ones**	nine

Represent numbers to 100

Pages 6–7

The place of each digit in a number tells us its value. Separating, or partitioning, numbers to 100 into tens and ones makes them easier to calculate.

We can use different objects, pictures and models to **partition** 2-digit numbers into tens and ones to show the **place value** of each **digit**.

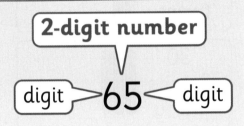

2-digit number

digit ➤ **65** ◄ digit

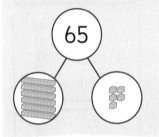

65

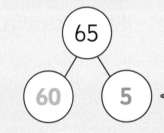

65

60   5

There are 6 tens and 5 ones
65 = 6 tens + 5 ones

To find the **value** of each digit, we look at its position in the place value chart.

To find the **whole number**, we **add** the values together.

60 + 5 = 65

The digit 6 is in the **tens** position.

The digit 5 is in the **ones** position.

10s	1s
6	5

The value of the 6 is 6 tens or 60.

The value of the 5 is 5 ones or 5.

This chart shows the number 65.

We can say:

10	20	30	40	50	(60)	70	80	90
1	2	3	4	(5)	6	7	8	9

There are 6 tens and 5 ones in 65.

We can also say:

65 **is equal to** 60 add 5.

Say Point to a number in the **tens** row, then a number in the **ones** row.

Say your number in different ways.

10	20	30	40	50	60	70	80	90
1	2	3	4	5	6	7	8	9

What numbers have been partitioned to show their place value?

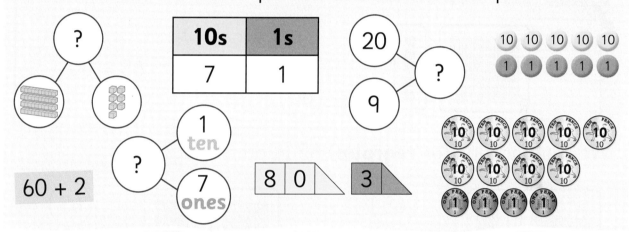

10s	1s
7	1

1 **ten**
7 **ones**

60 + 2

| 8 | 0 | / 3 |

11 to 100

Choose a number from 11 to 100.

How many different ways can you partition your number into **tens** and **ones**?

Build

What objects could you use?

Draw

What pictures or models might you draw?

Say

Which part shows the **ones**?

Which part shows the **tens**?

How many **tens** and **ones** are there?

Write

How would you write your number as an **addition number sentence**?

Pages 10–11, 14–17, 20–43

9

Represent numbers to 100 in different ways

Pages 6–9

We can partition numbers to 100 into tens and ones to show the place value of each digit. We can also partition 2-digit numbers in different ways.

Remember We can **partition** 65 into 60 and 5.

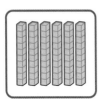  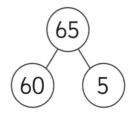

$$65 = 60 + 5$$

We can partition (or **regroup**) 65 in other ways.

  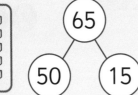

$$65 = 50 + 15$$

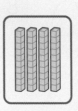 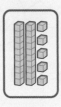 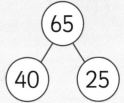

$$65 = 40 + 25$$

  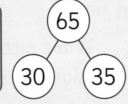

$$65 = 30 + 35$$

 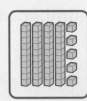 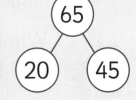

$$65 = 20 + 45$$

  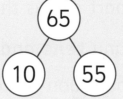

$$65 = 10 + 55$$

We can partition 42 into 40 and 2.

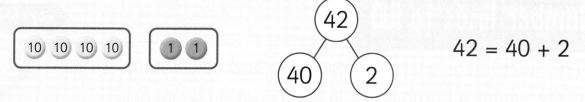

$$42 = 40 + 2$$

We can partition (or regroup) 42 in other ways.

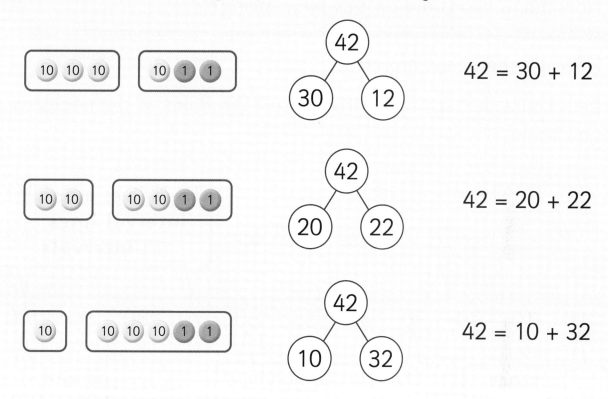

$$42 = 30 + 12$$

$$42 = 20 + 22$$

$$42 = 10 + 32$$

30 to 100

Choose a number from 30 to 100.

How many different ways can you partition (or regroup) your number?

 What objects could you use?

 What pictures or models might you draw?

 How would you write your number as an **addition number sentence**?

Pages 22–27, 30–43

Number lines to 100

Pages 6–7

A number line is useful for counting and calculating. It helps us see where a number lies in the counting sequence.

How many beads are on this bead string?

How are the beads grouped?

Let's count in steps of 10 from 0 to 100. Point to the beads as you count.

Look at this number line.

How is it the same as the bead string?

How is it different?

These lines are called **interval lines** or just **intervals**.

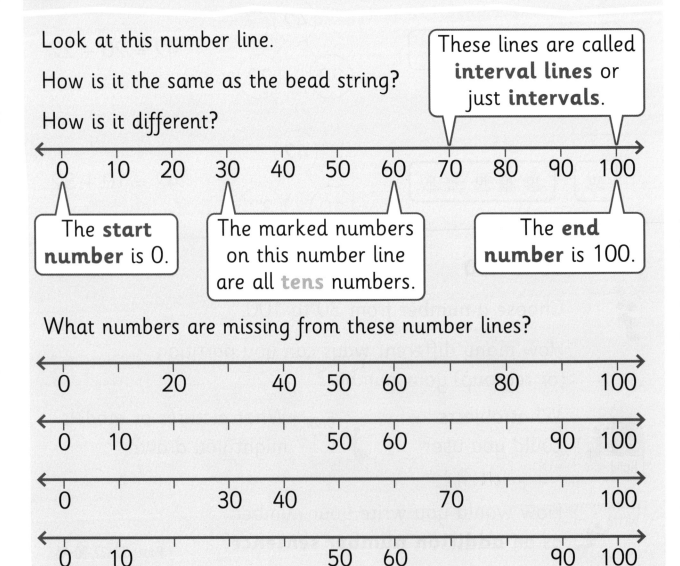

The **start number** is 0.

The marked numbers on this number line are all **tens** numbers.

The **end number** is 100.

What numbers are missing from these number lines?

0   20   40 50 60   80   100

0 10   50 60   90 100

0   30 40   70   100

0 10   50 60   90 100

What numbers are the arrows pointing to?

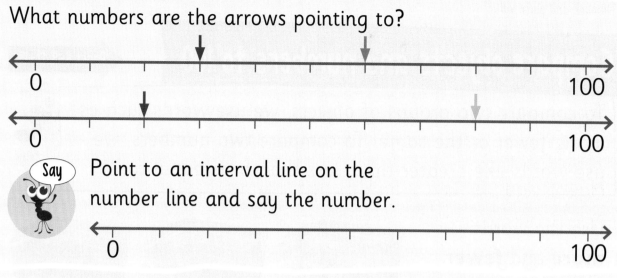

Say Point to an interval line on the
number line and say the number.

Look carefully at the start number and end
number on these number lines.

What numbers are the arrows pointing to?

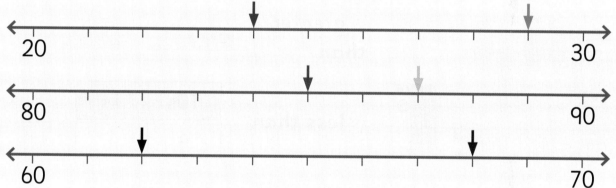

Look at this number line.

How is it the same as the number lines on page 12?

How is it different?

What numbers are the arrows pointing to on the number line?

For each of the numbers on the number line with an arrow
above it:

- what **tens** number comes **before** the number?
- what **tens** number comes **after** the number?

Pages 14-21

13

Compare objects and numbers to 100

Pages 6–9, 12–13

To compare two groups of objects, we use words such as more, fewer or the same. To compare two numbers, we use words like greater than, less than or is equal to.

Use the words **more** and **fewer** to **compare** these crates of fruit.

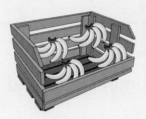  

We can use objects and models to represent and compare numbers.

 is **greater than**

| 6 | 0 | |

| 8 | |

 is **less than**

10s	1s
4	1

We can also use a number line to help compare two numbers.

22 is less than 41.

74 is greater than 68.

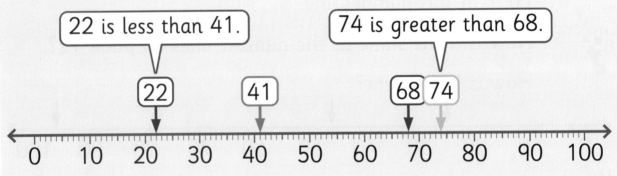

Use objects or models to show that:

Build **Draw**

| 27 is less than 36. | 53 is greater than 35. | 4 tens is **equal to** 40. |

We can also use **signs**, or **symbols**, to compare two numbers.

4 is greater than 2. 4 > 2

We can also say:

4 is **more than** 2.
4 is **larger than** 2.
4 > 2

2 is less than 4.
2 < 4

4 is equal to 4.
4 = 4

It's important to remember what each of these symbols mean.

greater than

less than

equal to

>

<

=

Look at the numbers marked on the number line on page 14. We can say and write:

74 is greater than 68

74 > 68

22 is less than 41

22 < 41

68 is equal to 68

68 = 68

Say
What **statements** can you make comparing pairs of marked numbers on this number line?

Write
Write these statements using the <, > and = symbols.

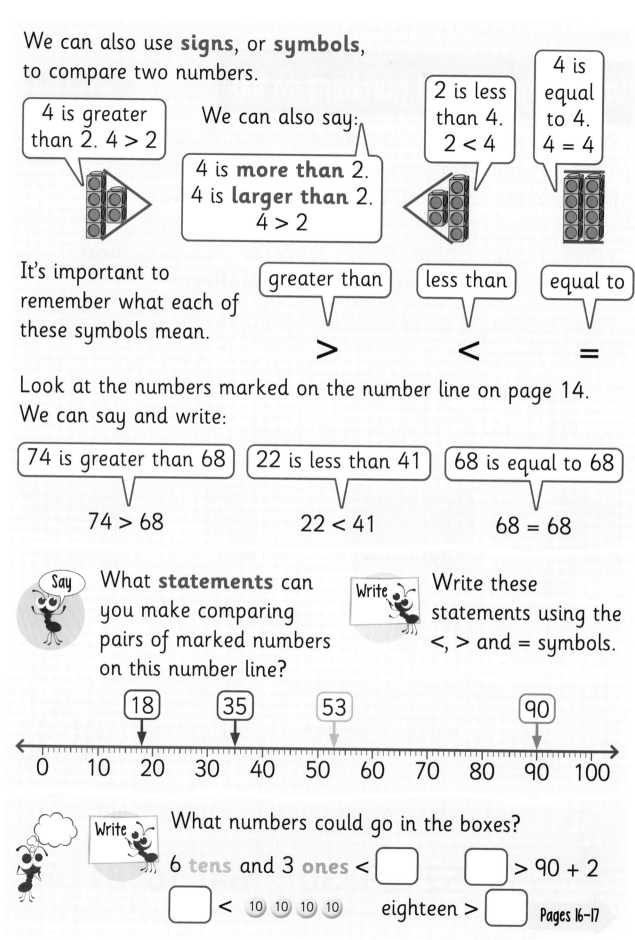

18   35   53   90

0 10 20 30 40 50 60 70 80 90 100

Write
What numbers could go in the boxes?

6 **tens** and 3 **ones** < ☐   ☐ > 90 + 2

☐ < 10 10 10 10   eighteen > ☐

Pages 16–17

Order objects and numbers to 100

Pages 6–9, 12–15

We can use what we know about comparing objects and numbers to order groups of objects or a set of numbers from smallest to largest, or from largest to smallest.

When ordering groups of objects, we use the words: **most**, **greatest**, **largest**, **least**, **fewest** or **smallest**.

When ordering a set of numbers, we use the words: greatest, largest or smallest.

Look at each group of Base 10.

We can **order** the numbers they represent from smallest to largest, or from largest to smallest.

 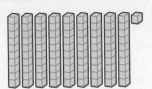 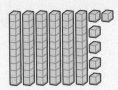

smallest to largest

| 28 | 43 | 66 | 91 |

largest to smallest

| 91 | 66 | 43 | 28 |

The four numbers above each have a different tens digit.

So, to order the numbers, we can just look at the tens digits.

 Say Order each set of numbers from smallest to largest.

| 13 | 52 | 29 | 30 | 64 | 16 | 81 | 46 |

Look at this set of numbers.

There are two numbers with the same **tens** digit.

89 58 64 84

So, to order this set of numbers, we need to look at their **ones** digits.

89 84

We can use **less than** signs to order the four numbers from smallest to largest:

58 < 64 < 84 < 89

Say Order each set of numbers. Start with the greatest number.

65 26 71 68

59 95 55 45

We can use a number line to order a set of numbers.

52 42 60 48

42 is the smallest number.

60 is the greatest number.

40 41 (42) 43 44 45 46 47 (48) 49 50 51 (52) 53 54 55 56 57 58 59 (60)

Write Order the numbers smallest to largest using less than symbols.

72 28 82 46 ☐ < ☐ < ☐ < ☐

Order the numbers largest to smallest using **greater than** symbols.

52 68 12 58 ☐ > ☐ > ☐ > ☐

Count in 2s, 3s, 5s and 10s

Pages 6–7, 12–13

Counting in steps of 2, 3, 5 and 10 involves recognising and continuing number patterns. Counting in steps – step counting – is important for multiplying or dividing.

Count in steps of 2

What do you notice about the numbers on this number line?

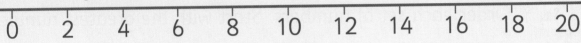

0 2 4 6 8 10 12 14 16 18 20

Say

- **Count on** from 0 to 20.
- **Count back** from 20 to 0.
- Starting from a number other than 0, count on in **2s** to 20.
- Starting from a number other than 20, count back in 2s to 0.

Use this 1–100 number square to count on and back in 2s.

1	2	3	4	5	6	7	8	9	10
11	12	13	14	15	16	17	18	19	20
21	22	23	24	25	26	27	28	29	30
31	32	33	34	35	36	37	38	39	40
41	42	43	44	45	46	47	48	49	50
51	52	53	54	55	56	57	58	59	60
61	62	63	64	65	66	67	68	69	70
71	72	73	74	75	76	77	78	79	80
81	82	83	84	85	86	87	88	89	90
91	92	93	94	95	96	97	98	99	100

Count in steps of 5

What do you notice about the numbers on this number line?

0 5 10 15 20 25 30 35 40 45 50

Say

- Count on from 0 to 50.
- Count back from 50 to 0.
- Starting from a number other than 0, count on in **5s** to 50.
- Starting from a number other than 50, count back in 5s to 0.

Use this 1–100 number square to count on and back in 5s.

1	2	3	4	5	6	7	8	9	10
11	12	13	14	15	16	17	18	19	20
21	22	23	24	25	26	27	28	29	30
31	32	33	34	35	36	37	38	39	40
41	42	43	44	45	46	47	48	49	50
51	52	53	54	55	56	57	58	59	60
61	62	63	64	65	66	67	68	69	70
71	72	73	74	75	76	77	78	79	80
81	82	83	84	85	86	87	88	89	90
91	92	93	94	95	96	97	98	99	100

Count in steps of 10

What do you notice about the numbers on this number line?

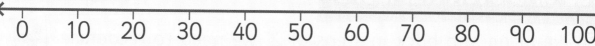

 **Say**
- Count on from 0 to 100.
- Count back from 100 to 0.
- Starting from a number other than 0, count on in **10s** to 100.
- Starting from a number other than 100, count back in 10s to 0.

Count in steps of 3

What do you notice about the numbers that are circled on this number line?

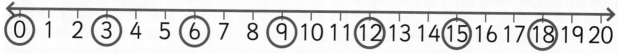

What do you notice about the numbers on this number line?

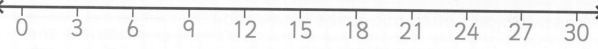

 Say
- Count on from 0 to 30.
- Count back from 30 to 0.
- Starting from a number other than 0, count on in **3s** to 30.
- Starting from a number other than 30, count back in 3s to 0.

Write Complete the number tracks.

6	9			21		

20			50		80	

40	35				10	

18		14	12			

Pages 20–21, 30–31, 36–39, 48–53

Odd and even numbers

Pages 6–9, 12–13, 18–19

To count on and back in steps of 2, we need to recognise and continue number patterns, including the patterns of odd and even numbers.

Look at the cubes under this number line.

Each set of cubes is made up of **groups of 2** cubes.

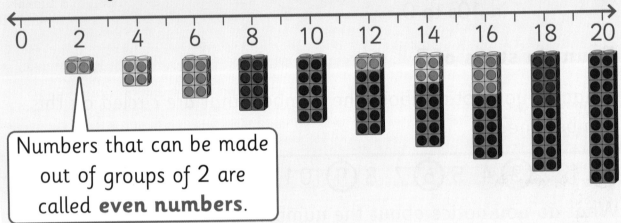

Numbers that can be made out of groups of 2 are called **even numbers**.

What do you notice about the **ones** digit in each of the even numbers?

Numbers that cannot be made out of groups of 2 are called **odd numbers**.

Look at the cubes under this number line.

What is different about these sets of cubes?

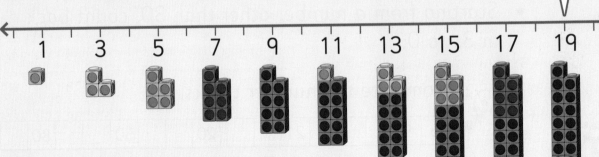

What do you notice about the **ones** digit in each of the odd numbers?

To tell whether a number is even or odd, look at the **ones** digit in the number.

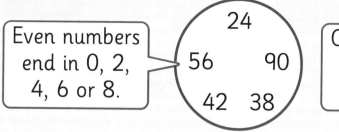

Even numbers end in 0, 2, 4, 6 or 8.

24
56   90
42   38

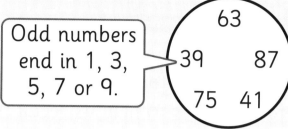

Odd numbers end in 1, 3, 5, 7 or 9.

63
39   87
75   41

Which of these numbers are even? Which are odd?

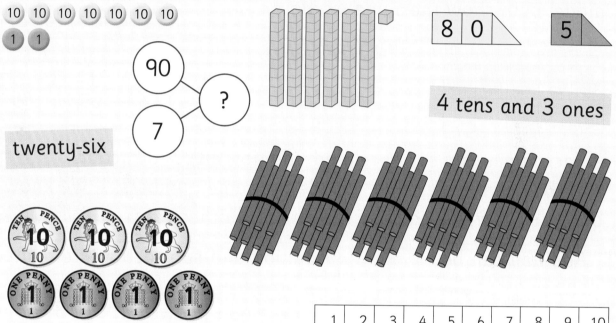

90
7
?

twenty-six

8 0

5

4 tens and 3 ones

10s	**1s**
5	8

50 + 9

Say Point to a number on the 1–100 number square and say whether it is even or odd.

1	2	3	4	5	6	7	8	9	10
11	12	13	14	15	16	17	18	19	20
21	22	23	24	25	26	27	28	29	30
31	32	33	34	35	36	37	38	39	40
41	42	43	44	45	46	47	48	49	50
51	52	53	54	55	56	57	58	59	60
61	62	63	64	65	66	67	68	69	70
71	72	73	74	75	76	77	78	79	80
81	82	83	84	85	86	87	88	89	90
91	92	93	94	95	96	97	98	99	100

Pages 48–49

Addition and subtraction facts to 10

Pages 6–9

Being able to recall addition and subtraction facts to 10 is important for solving other calculations. We can use fact families to help us recall these facts.

The ten frame and the part-whole model both show the same **addition** and **subtraction** facts.

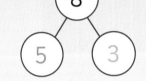

This is a **fact family** for 8.

5 + 3 = 8	8 − 3 = 5
3 + 5 = 8	8 − 5 = 3

A fact family is a set of related addition and subtraction **number sentences** that include the same numbers. If we know one **fact**, then we can use this to recall other **related facts**.

Addition can be done in any order.

So, 5 + 3 = 8 and 3 + 5 = 8

Addition and subtraction are related.

So, if you know that 5 + 3 = 8, you also know that 8 − 3 = 5 and that 8 − 5 = 3

Look at these other fact families for 8.

Say What addition and subtraction number sentences can you say for each fact family?

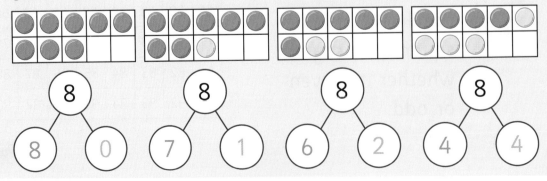

This bead string and part-whole model show a fact family for 6.

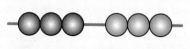

6 / 3 3

This addition fact is a **double**. Doubles can help us to recall some of the addition facts to 10.

 Say What addition and subtraction number sentences can you say for this fact family?

Can you think of any other fact families for 6?

 Build Use beads or other objects to build the fact families for 6.

 Draw How might you draw these fact families in a model?

 Write Write the related addition and subtraction number sentences for each fact family.

Knowing the fact families for 10 is important for solving other **calculations**.

Here are the related addition and subtraction number sentences for one fact family for 10.

10 / 7 3

$$7 + 3 = 10 \qquad 10 - 3 = 7$$
$$3 + 7 = 10 \qquad 10 - 7 = 3$$

This is a fact family for 10.

What are the other fact families for 10?

 Build **Draw** Use objects or draw models to show the fact families for 10.

 Say **Write** Say or write the related addition and subtraction number sentences for each fact family.

Pages 24–43

23

Addition and subtraction facts to 20

Pages 6–11, 22–23

Recalling the addition and subtraction facts to 10 helps with knowing the addition and subtraction facts to 20.

- **Addition** can be done in any order: put the **larger** number first and **count on**.
- Use **doubles** to help recall some addition facts to 20.

Remember

$8 + 6 = \boxed{14}$

8 + 6

10 **plus** 4 equals 14.

8 **add** 2 **equals** 10.

2   4

We can use a number line or ten frames.

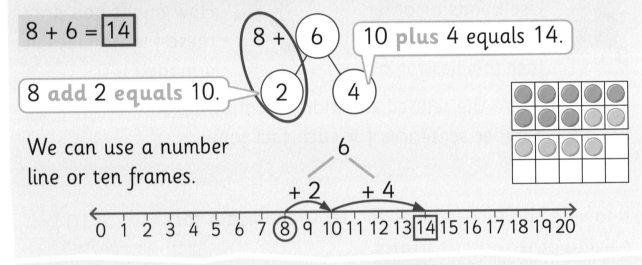

$13 + 4 = \boxed{17}$ **If** 3 + 4 = 7   **then**   13 + 4 = 17

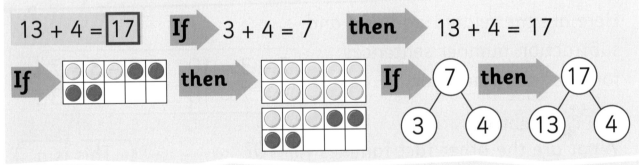

$3 + 14 = \boxed{17}$

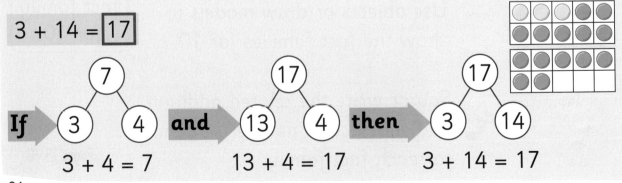

If 3   4   **and** 13   4   **then** 3   14

3 + 4 = 7   13 + 4 = 17   3 + 14 = 17

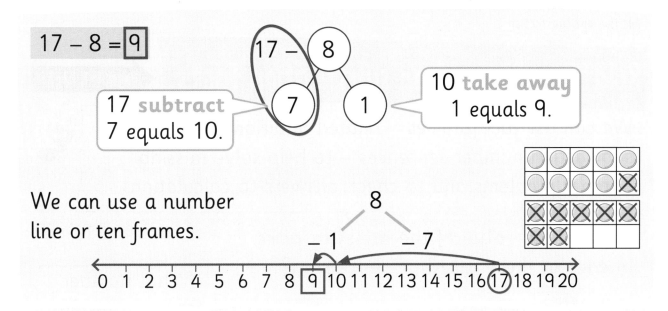

$17 - 8 = \boxed{9}$

17 – 8

7   1

17 **subtract** 7 equals 10.

10 **take away** 1 equals 9.

We can use a number line or ten frames.

8

– 1   – 7

0 1 2 3 4 5 6 7 8 $\boxed{9}$ 10 11 12 13 14 15 16 17 18 19 20

 Remember   We can think of subtraction as finding the difference, which means comparing the number of objects in one set with the number of objects in another set.

$15 - 7 = \boxed{8}$

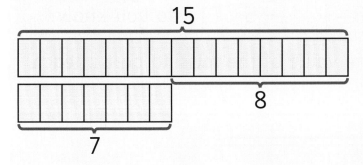

15	
7	8

 Build   Use objects to build each of these addition and subtraction facts to 20.

 Draw   How might you draw each of these in a model?

13 + 6 = ☐   18 – 7 = ☐

9 + 7 = ☐   16 – 9 = ☐

Pages 26–43

Related addition and subtraction facts

Pages 6–11, 22–25

We can use fact families – related addition and subtraction number sentences – to help solve missing number problems and to check answers to calculations.

What is the **value** of the **missing part** in each of these **number sentences**?

We know the **whole**.

We know one **part**.

What number are we **counting on** from? How do you know?

The other part is missing.

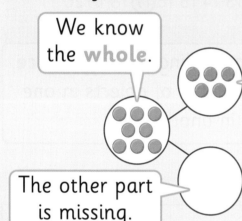

$5 + \boxed{} = 8$

$8 - \boxed{} = 5$

What number are we **counting back** from? How do you know?

How would you work out the value of the missing part in each of these number sentences?

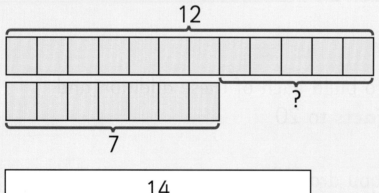

12

7

?

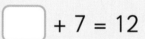

$\boxed{} + 7 = 12$

$12 - \boxed{} = 7$

14	
9	?

$9 + \boxed{} = 14$

$14 - \boxed{} = 9$

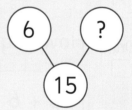

$\boxed{} + 6 = 15$

$15 - \boxed{} = 6$

Addition and **subtraction** are **inverse operations**.

Addition, subtraction, multiplication and division are all **operations**.

That means that they are **opposite operations**. Addition **reverses** subtraction, and subtraction reverses addition.

We can use the **inverse relationship** between addition and subtraction to help solve missing number problems.

Work out the value of the missing part in these number sentences.

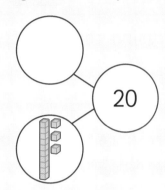
20

13 + ☐ = 20

20 – 13 = ☐

☐ + 13 = 20

20 – ☐ = 13

We can also use **fact families** and the inverse relationship between addition and subtraction to **check the answers** to **calculations**.

Dillon does this calculation: 17 – 5 = 12

Which of the following could he use to check his answer?

17	
5	

5 + 12   17 – 12

12 – 5   12 + 5

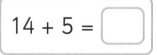
14 + 5 = ☐

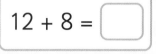
18 – 6 = ☐

12 + 8 = ☐

19 – 8 = ☐

Work out the answer to each calculation.

Then draw a model or write a number sentence to check your answers.

Pages 28–43

Add three 1-digit numbers

Pages 6–9, 22–27

It is often useful to add more than two numbers.

Sami rolls three dice.

What is Sami's **total** roll?

We can show this using ten frames.

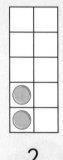  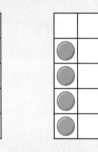 **leads to**

2 + 5 + 4 = 11

We can also show this using a bar model or a part-whole model.

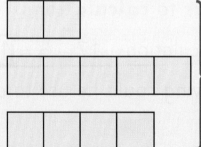 } 11

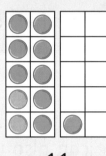

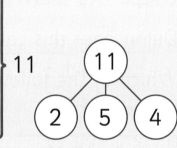

11		
2	5	4

We can use a number line to help **add** three **1-digit numbers**.

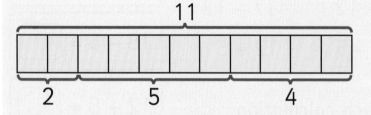

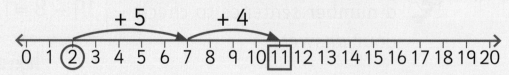

Lisa rolls these three dice.

What is Lisa's total roll?

When **adding** together three or more 1-digit numbers, it's important to look at the numbers and decide the best way to work out the answer.

- Put the **larger** number first.

> **Addition** can be done in any order. `Remember`

$$+ 5 \qquad + 4$$

0 1 2 3 4 5 ⑥ 7 8 9 10 11 12 13 14 [15] 16 17 18 19 20

- Look for pairs of numbers that total 10.

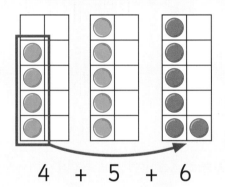

4 + 6 = 10

leads to

10 + 5 = 15

4 + 5 + 6 = 15

If you change the order of the numbers, the total will still be the same.

4 + 5 + 6 = 15
6 + 5 + 4 = 15
6 + 4 + 5 = 15
4 + 6 + 5 = 15

Which of these **number sentences** do you think is the easiest? Why?

> `Remember` Use **doubles** to help recall addition facts.

What is the total roll of the four dice?

Build **Draw** Use objects or draw a model to work out the answer.

Write What number sentence will you write?

Pages 40–41

Add and subtract 10s

Pages 6–11, 18–19, 22–27

Being able to recall the addition and subtraction facts to 10 helps us to add and subtract tens (10s) numbers, such as 50 + 30 or 70 – 30.

$$50 + 30 = \boxed{80}$$

We can use the known **fact**
5 + 3 = 8 to help us.

Change the **ones** to **tens**.

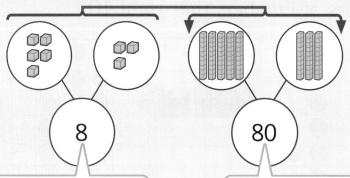

If we know that:
5 **ones** + 3 **ones** = 8 **ones**
5 + 3 = 8

we also know that:
5 **tens** + 3 **tens** = 8 **tens**
50 + 30 = 80

- **Addition** can be done in any order.
- **Fact families** – that addition and **subtraction** are related. If we know one addition or subtraction fact, then we know three other **related facts**.

Remember

So,

5 + 3 = 8	50 + 30 = 80
3 + 5 = 8	30 + 50 = 80
8 – 3 = 5	80 – 30 = 50
8 – 5 = 3	80 – 50 = 30

and

$70 - 30 = \boxed{40}$ < We can use the known fact
$7 - 3 = 4$.

Change the **ones** to **tens**.

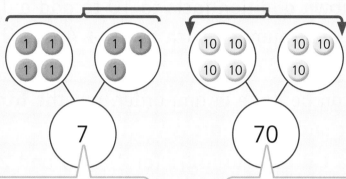

| 7 ones $- 3$ ones $= 4$ ones
$7 - 3 = 4$ | **so** | 7 tens $- 3$ tens $= 4$ tens
$70 - 30 = 40$ |

Say If you know that $70 - 30 = 40$, what other addition and subtraction facts do you know?

Complete the part-whole models and the missing numbers in these **calculations**.

$6 + \boxed{} = 10$	$60 + \boxed{} = 100$
$\boxed{} + 6 = 10$	$\boxed{} + 60 = 100$
$10 - \boxed{} = 6$	$100 - \boxed{} = 60$
$10 - 6 = \boxed{}$	$100 - 60 = \boxed{}$

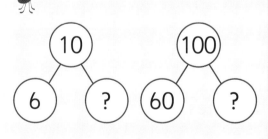

Build **Draw** Use objects or draw a model to show answers to these calculations.

$20 + 40 = \boxed{}$

$90 - 50 = \boxed{}$

Write If you know each of these answers, what other related facts do you know?

Pages 36–43

31

Add a 2-digit number and 1s

Pages 6–11, 22–27

We can use known addition facts to 10 to add a 1-digit number to a 2-digit number, such as 35 + 4 and 27 + 8.

- **Addition** can be done in any order: put the **larger** number first and **count on**. | Remember
- 4 and 8 are **1-digit numbers** (or 1s). 35 and 27 are **2-digit numbers**.

$35 + 4 = \boxed{39}$

We can use the known fact 5 + 4 = 9 to help.

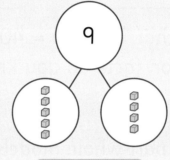

So, $\boxed{5 + 4 = 9}$ and

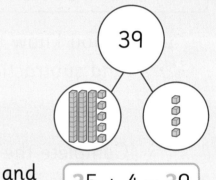

$\boxed{35 + 4 = 39}$

What's the same about these two **calculations**?

What's different?

What do you notice about these number lines?

What stays the same? What changes?

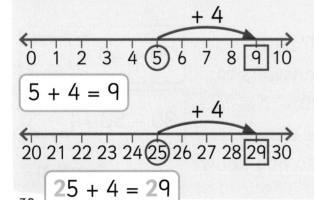

$5 + 4 = 9$

$25 + 4 = 29$

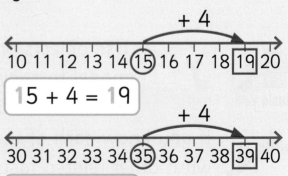

$15 + 4 = 19$

$35 + 4 = 39$

$27 + 8 = \boxed{35}$

We can work this out in different ways.

10 **ones** is equal to 1 **ten**. = Remember

- Base 10 or place value counters

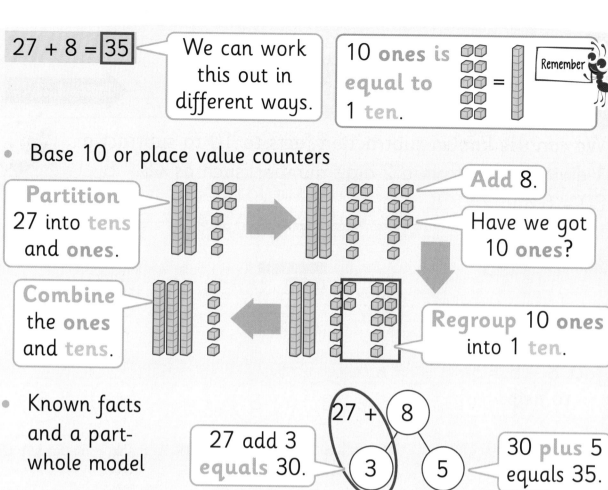

Partition 27 into **tens** and **ones**.

Add 8.

Have we got 10 **ones**?

Combine the **ones** and **tens**.

Regroup 10 **ones** into 1 **ten**.

- Known facts and a part-whole model

27 add 3 **equals** 30.

$27 +$ 8

3 5

30 **plus** 5 equals 35.

- Number line

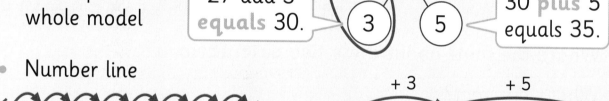

27 28 29 30 31 32 33 34 35 or $+ 3$ $+ 5$ 27 30 35

- Place value chart

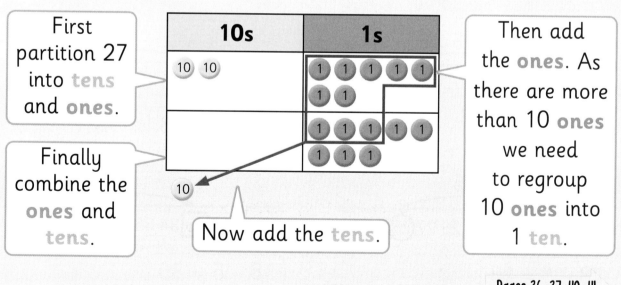

First partition 27 into **tens** and **ones**.

10s	**1s**

Then add the **ones**. As there are more than 10 **ones** we need to regroup 10 **ones** into 1 **ten**.

Finally combine the **ones** and **tens**.

Now add the **tens**.

Pages 36–37, 40–41

Subtract a 2-digit number and 1s

Pages 6–11, 22–27

We can use known subtraction facts to 10 to subtract a 1-digit number from a 2-digit number, such as 48 − 5, 80 − 6 and 24 − 8.

48 − 5 = 43

We can use the known fact 8 − 5 = 3 to help.

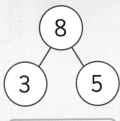

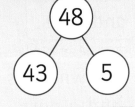

So, 8 − 5 = 3 and 48 − 5 = 43

What's the same about these two **calculations**?

What's different?

What do you notice about these number lines?

What stays the same? What changes?

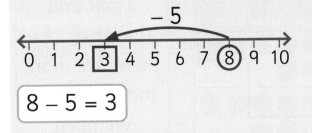

8 − 5 = 3

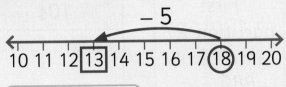

18 − 5 = 13

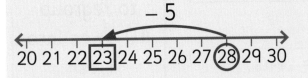

28 − 5 = 23

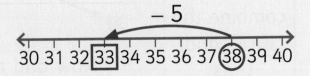

38 − 5 = 33

$80 - 6 = \boxed{74}$

We can use a number line or 1–100 number square to answer this calculation.

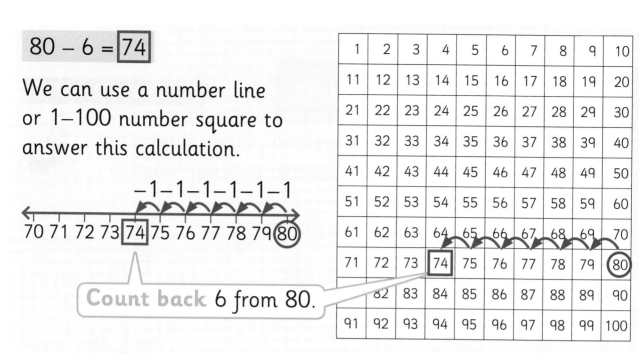

$-1-1-1-1-1-1$

70 71 72 73 |74| 75 76 77 78 79 (80)

Count back 6 from 80.

1	2	3	4	5	6	7	8	9	10
11	12	13	14	15	16	17	18	19	20
21	22	23	24	25	26	27	28	29	30
31	32	33	34	35	36	37	38	39	40
41	42	43	44	45	46	47	48	49	50
51	52	53	54	55	56	57	58	59	60
61	62	63	64	65	66	67	68	69	70
71	72	73	74	75	76	77	78	79	80
81	82	83	84	85	86	87	88	89	90
91	92	93	94	95	96	97	98	99	100

$24 - 8 = \boxed{16}$ ← We can work this out in different ways.

- Known facts and a part-whole model

24 subtract 4 equals 20.

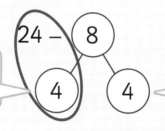

20 take away 4 equals 16.

- Number line

16 17 18 19 20 21 22 23 24   or

-4 -4

16   20   24

- Place value chart

First partition 24 into tens and ones.

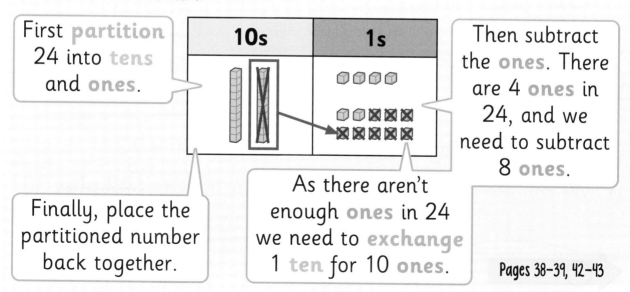

10s	1s

Then subtract the ones. There are 4 ones in 24, and we need to subtract 8 ones.

As there aren't enough ones in 24 we need to exchange 1 ten for 10 ones.

Finally, place the partitioned number back together.

Pages 38–39, 42–43

Add a 2-digit number and 10s

Pages 6–11, 18–19, 22–27, 30–33

We can use known addition facts and place value to help us to add a tens (10s) number to a 2-digit number, such as 42 + 30.

42 + 30 = $\boxed{72}$

42 **is equal to** 4 **tens** and 2 **ones**.

3 **tens**.

7 **tens add** 2 **ones** is equal to 72. 70 + 2 = 72

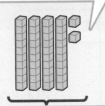

leads to

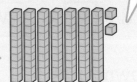

We know that 4 + 3 = 7.
So, 4 **tens** + 3 **tens** = 7 **tens**.
40 + 30 = 70

What do you notice about the **tens** digits? What about the **ones** digits?

What changes when we add a **tens** number? What stays the same?

We can use known facts and a part-whole model.

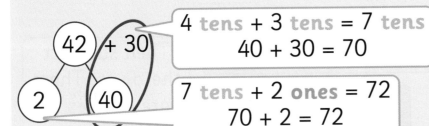

4 **tens** + 3 **tens** = 7 **tens**
40 + 30 = 70

7 **tens** + 2 **ones** = 72
70 + 2 = 72

Addition can be done in any order.

Remember

There are other ways we can work out 42 + 30 = 72.

- We can use a number line to **count on in tens**.

42 **plus** 30 **equals** 72.

+ 10   + 10   + 10

(42)   52   62 $\boxed{72}$

- We can use a 1–100 number square to count on in tens.

1	2	3	4	5	6	7	8	9	10
11	12	13	14	15	16	17	18	19	20
21	22	23	24	25	26	27	28	29	30
31	32	33	34	35	36	37	38	39	40
41	42	43	44	45	46	47	48	49	50
51	52	53	54	55	56	57	58	59	60
61	62	63	64	65	66	67	68	69	70
71	72	73	74	75	76	77	78	79	80
81	82	83	84	85	86	87	88	89	90
91	92	93	94	95	96	97	98	99	100

42 + 10

52 + 10

62 + 10

- We can use a place value chart.

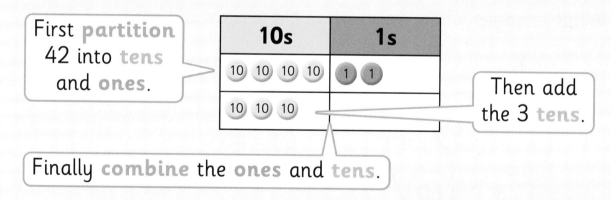

First **partition** 42 into **tens** and **ones**.

Then add the 3 **tens**.

Finally **combine** the **ones** and **tens**.

What do you notice about these part-whole models?

What stays the same? What changes?

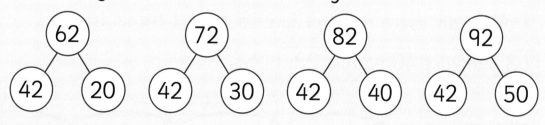

Pages 40–41

Subtract a 2-digit number and 10s

Pages 6–11, 18–19, 22–27, 30–31, 34–35

We can use known subtraction facts and place value to help us to subtract a tens (10s) number from a 2-digit number, such as 63 – 40.

63 – 40 = 23

63 **is equal to** 6 **tens** and 3 **ones**.

2 **tens** add 3 **ones** equals 23. 20 + 3 = 23

We know that 6 – 4 = 2. So, 6 **tens** – 4 **tens** = 2 **tens**. 60 – 40 = 20

What do you notice about the **tens** digits? What about the **ones** digits?

What changes when we **subtract** a **tens** number? What stays the same?

We can use known facts and a part-whole model.

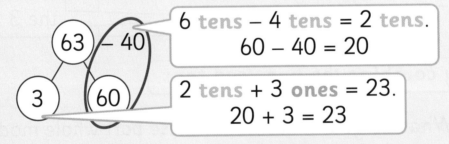

63 – 40

3   60

6 **tens** – 4 **tens** = 2 **tens**. 60 – 40 = 20

2 **tens** + 3 **ones** = 23. 20 + 3 = 23

There are other ways we can work out 63 – 40 = 23.

• We can use a number line to **count back in tens**.

63 subtract 40 equals 23.

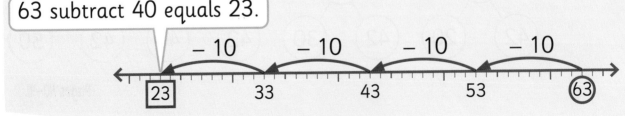

– 10   – 10   – 10   – 10

23   33   43   53   63

- We can use a 1–100 number square to count back in tens.

1	2	3	4	5	6	7	8	9	10
11	12	13	14	15	16	17	18	19	20
21	22	23	24	25	26	27	28	29	30
31	32	33	34	35	36	37	38	39	40
41	42	43	44	45	46	47	48	49	50
51	52	53	54	55	56	57	58	59	60
61	62	63	64	65	66	67	68	69	70
71	72	73	74	75	76	77	78	79	80
81	82	83	84	85	86	87	88	89	90
91	92	93	94	95	96	97	98	99	100

33 – 10

43 – 10

53 – 10

63 – 10

- We can use a place value chart.

10s	1s

First **partition** 63 into **tens** and **ones**.

Then subtract the 4 **tens**.

Finally place the partitioned number back together.

What do you notice about these part-whole models?

What stays the same? What changes?

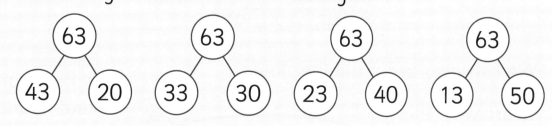

Pages 42–43

Add two 2-digit numbers

Pages 6–11, 22–33, 36–37

Adding two 2-digit numbers involves partitioning the numbers into tens and ones, and recalling addition facts to 20.

62 + 35 = 97

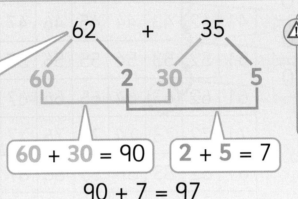

Partition both numbers into **tens** and **ones**.

60 + 30 = 90   2 + 5 = 7

90 + 7 = 97

⚠ **ALWAYS:**

Estimate
Calculate
Check

In the example above, we partitioned both numbers into **tens** and **ones**.

In the example below, we are only going to partition one number into **tens** and **ones**.

Partition 62 into **tens** and **ones**.

62 + 35

60   2

60 + 35 = 95

95 + 2 = 97

Addition can be done in any order.

Remember

So, partitioning the **larger** number makes the **calculation** easier.

- What's the same about these two methods?
- What's different?
- Which do you think is better?
- Why?

We can also use a number line.

Start with the larger number.

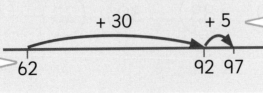

+ 30   + 5

62   92 97

Partition 35 and count on in **tens** and **ones**.

$46 + 27 = \boxed{73}$ **Partition both numbers or just one number.**

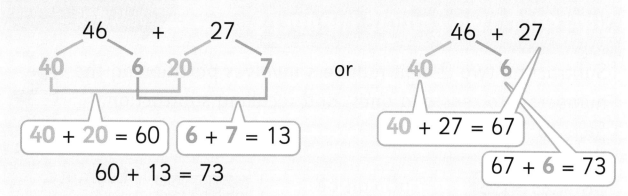

$46 + 27$

$40 \quad 6 \quad 20 \quad 7$

$\boxed{40 + 20 = 60}$ $\boxed{6 + 7 = 13}$

$60 + 13 = 73$

or

$46 + 27$

$40 \quad 6$

$\boxed{40 + 27 = 67}$

$\boxed{67 + 6 = 73}$

We can also use a number line to work out the answer.

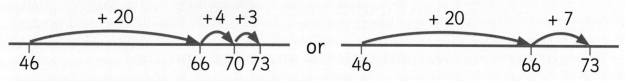

$+20 \qquad +4 \ +3$

46 \qquad 66 \ 70 \ 73

or

$+20 \qquad +7$

46 \qquad 66 \qquad 73

In the calculation $46 + 27$, the **ones digits** add up to more than 10. $\boxed{6 + 7 = 13}$

So, we have to **regroup** 10 **ones** into 1 **ten**. $\boxed{\text{1 ten and 3 ones}}$

We can show this using a place value chart.

First partition both numbers into tens and ones.

Finally combine the ones and tens.

Now add the tens.

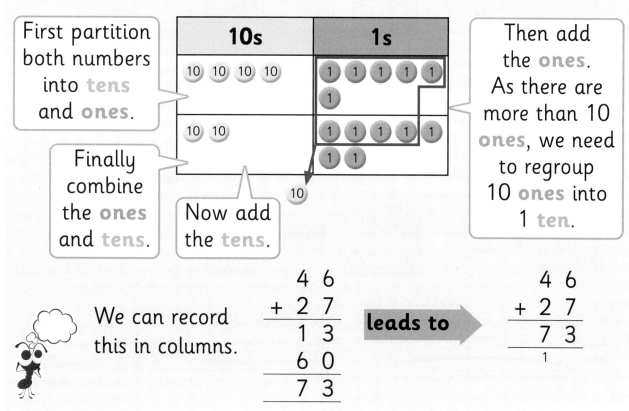

Then add the ones. As there are more than 10 ones, we need to regroup 10 ones into 1 ten.

We can record this in columns.

```
  4 6
+ 2 7
-----
  1 3
  6 0
-----
  7 3
```

leads to

```
  4 6
+ 2 7
-----
  7 3
  1
```

41

Subtract two 2-digit numbers

Pages 6–11, 22–27, 30–31, 34–35, 38–39

Subtracting two 2-digit numbers involves partitioning the numbers into tens and ones, and recalling subtraction facts to 10.

⚠ **ALWAYS:**
Estimate
Calculate
Check

$58 - 23 = \boxed{35}$

58 can be **partitioned** into 5 **tens** and 8 **ones**.

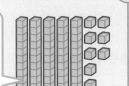

To **subtract** 23, we partition 23 into **tens** and **ones**.

We first subtract the **tens**, and then the **ones**.

| Begin by subtracting 2 **tens** (20) … | … and then 3 **ones**. | 3 **tens** + 5 **ones** = 35
 30 + 5 = 35 |

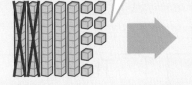 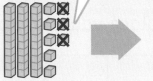 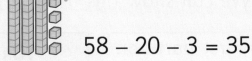

$58 - 20 - 3 = 35$

We can also work out the answer by first subtracting the **ones**, and then the **tens**.

| Begin by subtracting 3 **ones** … | … and then 2 **tens** (20). | 3 **tens** + 5 **ones** = 35
 30 + 5 = 35 |

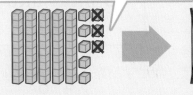 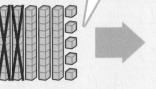 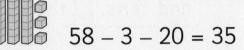

$58 - 3 - 20 = 35$

We can use a number line for each method.

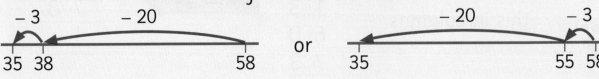

or

$42 - 25 = \boxed{17}$

Partition 42 into **tens** and **ones**.

Partition 25 into **tens** and **ones**.

We can't subtract the **ones**. But we can partition 42 a different way.

$$\begin{array}{cc} & 42 \\ 4\ 0 & 2 \\ -\ 2\ 0 & -\ 5 \end{array}$$

Here we partition 42 into **30** and **12**.

We keep 25 partitioned into **tens** and **ones**.

Now we can subtract the **tens** and the **ones** and combine the partitioned number into 17.

$$\begin{array}{cc} & 42 \\ 3\ 0 & 1\ 2 \\ -\ 2\ 0 & -\ 5 \\ \hline 1\ 0 & 7 \end{array}$$

We can show this using a place value chart.

First partition 42 into **tens** and **ones**.

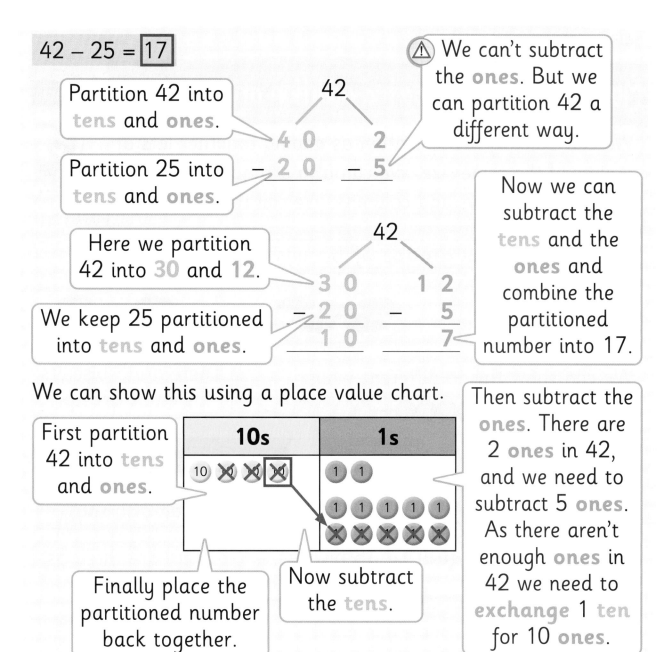

10s	1s

Now subtract the **tens**.

Finally place the partitioned number back together.

Then subtract the **ones**. There are 2 **ones** in 42, and we need to subtract 5 **ones**. As there aren't enough **ones** in 42 we need to **exchange** 1 **ten** for 10 **ones**.

We can record this in columns.

$$\begin{array}{cc} {}^{30}\ \cancel{40} & {}^{12}\ \cancel{2} \\ -\ 20 & 5 \\ \hline 10 & 7 \\ \hline \multicolumn{2}{c}{10 + 7 = 17} \end{array}$$

leads to

$$\begin{array}{c} {}^{3}\ {}^{1} \\ \cancel{4}\ 2 \\ -\ 2\ 5 \\ \hline 1\ 7 \end{array}$$

$$\begin{array}{c} {}^{3}\ {}^{12} \\ \cancel{4}\ 2 \\ -\ 2\ 5 \\ \hline 1\ 7 \end{array}$$

We can also write the exchanged values like this.

We can also use a number line.

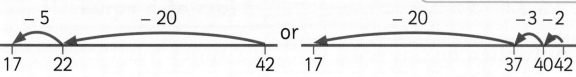

or

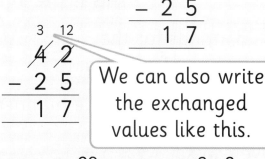

Multiplication as repeated addition and an array Pages 6–7

We can think of multiplication as adding together lots of groups of the same size. We can also arrange groups of the same size into rows and columns. We call this an array.

There are 3 **equal groups of** biscuits.

We can show this in different ways:

There are 5 biscuits **in each group**.

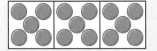 

We can say:

There are 3 groups of 5 biscuits, which **is equal to** 15 biscuits.

We can also say:

There are three 5s.

We can write this as an **addition number sentence**:

5 + 5 + 5 = 15

We can also write this as a **multiplication number sentence**:

3 × 5 = 15

This is the **symbol** for multiplication.

3 stands for the **number of groups**.

3 × 5 = 15

15 stands for the **total number** of biscuits.

5 stands for the number of biscuits in each group.

We can say: 3 × 5 = 15

3 lots of 5 equals 15.

3 **multiplied by** 5 is equal to 15.   3 **times** 5 is 15.

This **array** shows 4 lots of 5 cars.

$$5 + 5 + 5 + 5 = 20$$

$$4 \times 5 = 20$$

It also shows 5 lots of 4 cars.

$$4 + 4 + 4 + 4 + 4 = 20$$

$$5 \times 4 = 20$$

We can see from this array that:
4 lots of 5 = 5 lots of 4
$4 \times 5 = 5 \times 4$

We can show this array in different ways:

An array shows us that multiplication can be done in any order.

 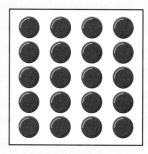

What does this picture show?

Remember Think about **counting in steps** of 2.

 What objects could you use to show this?

 Draw How might you draw this in a model? Can you draw this as an array?

 Write How would you write this as an addition number sentence? How would you write this as a multiplication number sentence?

Pages 48–53

Division as sharing and grouping

Pages 6–7

Division involves separating a group of objects – the whole – into smaller equal groups or parts.

Division as sharing

Division as sharing is when a group of objects is **shared equally between** a known **number of groups**, and we need to find out how many objects belong **in each group**.

There were 15 biscuits in the box.
They were shared equally between 3 plates.
There are 5 biscuits on each plate.

We can say: 15 **divided between** 3 **is equal to** 5 each.

We can also say: 15 shared equally between 3 is 5.

15 **shared between** 3 is 5.

We can show this in a model:

15

We can write this as a **division number sentence**: 15 ÷ 3 = 5

This is the **symbol** for division.

15 stands for the **total number** of biscuits.

15 ÷ 3 = 5

5 stands for the number of biscuits in each group.

3 stands for the number of groups.

We can say:
15 ÷ 3 = 5

15 divided between 3 **equals** 5.

15 **divided by** 3 is equal to 5.

Division as grouping

We can think of division like this: We know the total number of objects. We know how many objects belong in each group. We need to find out how many **equal groups** there are.

Yua had 12 seeds.

She planted 2 seeds in each pot.

She used 6 pots.

We can say:

12 has been **divided into groups of** 2. There are 6 groups.

We can also say: There are 6 equal groups of 2 in 12.

We can show this in a model:

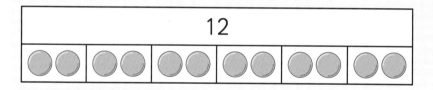

We can write this as a division number sentence: $12 \div 2 = 6$

This is the symbol for division.

12 stands for the total number of seeds.

$12 \div 2 = 6$

6 stands for the number of groups.

2 stands for the number of seeds in each group.

We can say: $12 \div 2 = 6$

12 divided by 2 is equal to 6.

12 divided into groups of 2 equals 6.

Pages 48–61

2 multiplication table

Pages 6–7, 18–21, 44–47

We can use the pattern of counting in steps of 2 to recall the 2 multiplication table facts and the related division facts.

How many flowers are there **altogether**?

We can **count on in twos** to find out how many flowers there are.

1 **group of** 2 is 2.

3 groups of 2 are 6.

There are 4 groups of 2 flowers. There are 8 flowers altogether.

0   2   4   6   8   10   12   14   16   18   20   22   24

2 groups of 2 are 4.

4 groups of 2 are 8.

We can also write this as a multiplication **number sentence**:

$4 \times 2 = 8$

4 **lots of** 2 is 8.

4 **multiplied by** 2 equals 8.

We can say:

The **product** of 4 and 2 is 8.

4 **times** 2 is 8.

Four **2s** are 8.

Look at this pattern. Can you continue the pattern?

Look at the 1–100 number square on page 18 to help you count in 2s.

Remember

 One 2 is 2. $1 \times 2 = 2$

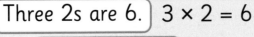 Two 2s are 4. $2 \times 2 = 4$

Three 2s are 6. $3 \times 2 = 6$

 Four 2s are 8. $4 \times 2 = 8$

 Five 2s are 10. $5 \times 2 = 10$

Multiplication and **division** are related.

They are **inverse operations**.

Addition, subtraction, multiplication and division are all **operations**.

Remember

That means that they are **opposite operations** – multiplication **reverses** division, and division reverses multiplication.

We can use the **inverse relationship** between multiplication and division to help us recall the **division facts** related to the 2 **multiplication table facts**.

There are 8 flowers altogether.

There are 2 flowers in each pot.

There are 4 pots.

As a division we can say: 8 **divided by** 2 is equal to 4.

We can write this as: 8 ÷ 2 = 4

We can use this number line to help us recall the 2 multiplication table facts and the related division facts.

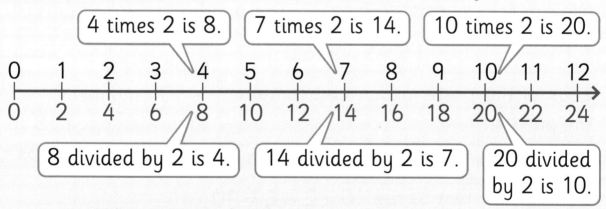

4 times 2 is 8.

7 times 2 is 14.

10 times 2 is 20.

8 divided by 2 is 4.

14 divided by 2 is 7.

20 divided by 2 is 10.

Is there a link between the 2 multiplication table and **doubling**?

What about between dividing by 2 and **halving**?

Pages 50–55

5 multiplication table

Pages 6–7, 18–19, 44–49

We can use the pattern of counting in steps of 5 to recall the 5 multiplication table facts and the related division facts.

How many fingers are there **altogether**?

We can **count on in fives** to find out how many fingers there are.

| 1 **group** of 5 is 5. | 3 groups of 5 are 15. | 5 groups of 5 are 25. | There are 6 groups of 5 fingers. There are 30 fingers altogether. |

| 2 groups of 5 are 10. | 4 groups of 5 are 20. | 6 groups of 5 are 30. |

0 5 10 15 20 25 30 35 40 45 50 55 60

We can also write this as a multiplication **number sentence**:

$6 \times 5 = 30$ 6 **lots of** 5 equals 30.   6 **multiplied by** 5 is 30.

We can say: The **product** of 6 and 5 is 30.

6 **times** 5 is 30.   Six **5s** are 30.

Look at this pattern. Can you continue the pattern?

> **Remember**
> Look at the 1–100 number square on page 18 to help you count in 5s.

 One 5 is 5. $1 \times 5 = 5$

 Two 5s are 10. $2 \times 5 = 10$

 Three 5s are 15. $3 \times 5 = 15$

 Four 5s are 20. $4 \times 5 = 20$

Five 5s are 25. $5 \times 5 = 25$

Multiplication and **division** are related. They are **inverse operations** – multiplication **reverses** division, and division reverses multiplication.

We can use the **inverse relationship** between multiplication and division to help us recall the **division facts** related to the 5 **multiplication table facts**.

There are 30 fingers altogether.

Each hand has 5 fingers.

There are 6 hands.

As a division we can say: 30 **divided by** 5 equals 6.

We can write this as: $30 \div 5 = 6$

We can use this number line to help us recall the 5 multiplication table facts and the related division facts.

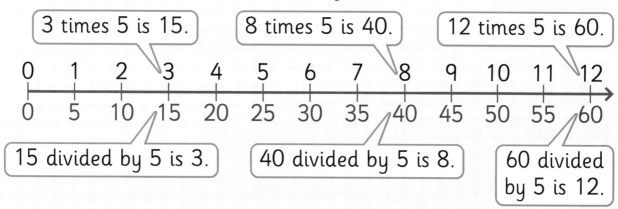

3 times 5 is 15.

8 times 5 is 40.

12 times 5 is 60.

15 divided by 5 is 3.

40 divided by 5 is 8.

60 divided by 5 is 12.

What do you notice about these **statements**?

What's the same? $6 \times 5 = 5 \times 6$ $2 \times 5 = 5 \times 2$

What's different? $2 \times 10 = 10 \times 2$

What does this tell us about multiplication?

Pages 52–53

10 multiplication table

Pages 6–7, 18–19, 44–51

We can use the pattern of counting in steps of 10 to recall the 10 multiplication table facts and the related division facts.

How many eggs are there **altogether**?

We can **count on in tens** to find out how many eggs there are.

| 1 **group of** 10 is 10. | 3 groups of 10 are 30. | 5 groups of 10 are 50. | There are 5 groups of 10 eggs. There are 50 eggs altogether. |

0 10 20 30 40 50 60 70 80 90 100 110 120

2 groups of 10 are 20.

4 groups of 10 are 40.

We can also write this as a multiplication **number sentence**:
5 × 10 = 50

5 **lots of** 10 is 50.   5 **multiplied by** 10 is 50.

We can say:

The **product** of 5 and 10 is 50.

5 **times** 10 equals 50.   Five **10s** are 50.

  One 10 is 10. 1 × 10 = 10

Two 10s are 20. 2 × 10 = 20

Three 10s are 30. 3 × 10 = 30

Four 10s are 40. 4 × 10 = 40

 Five 10s are 50. 5 × 10 = 50

We can use the **inverse relationship** between multiplication and division to help us recall the **division facts** related to the 10 **multiplication table facts**.

Remember

Altogether there are 50 eggs.

There are 10 eggs in each carton.

There are 5 cartons.

As a division we can say: 50 **divided by** 10 is 5.

We can write this as: 50 ÷ 10 = 5

We can use this number line to help us recall the
10 multiplication table facts and the related division facts.

2 times 10 is 20.

6 times 10 is 60.

9 times 10 is 90.

0	1	2	3	4	5	6	7	8	9	10	11	12
0	10	20	30	40	50	60	70	80	90	100	110	120

20 divided by 10 is 2.

60 divided by 10 is 6.

90 divided by 10 is 9.

Look at this 1–100 number square.

How can you use this number square to help you recall the 10 multiplication table facts and the related division facts?

1	2	3	4	5	6	7	8	9	10
11	12	13	14	15	16	17	18	19	20
21	22	23	24	25	26	27	28	29	30
31	32	33	34	35	36	37	38	39	40
41	42	43	44	45	46	47	48	49	50
51	52	53	54	55	56	57	58	59	60
61	62	63	64	65	66	67	68	69	70
71	72	73	74	75	76	77	78	79	80
81	82	83	84	85	86	87	88	89	90
91	92	93	94	95	96	97	98	99	100

53

Half

Pages 6–7, 46–49

A fraction is part of a whole. A half means one of two equal parts.

Each of these shapes and objects show **one-half** or a **half**.

Each part is one-half of the **whole**.

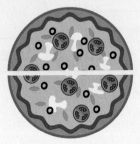

The whole has been **divided into** 2 **equal parts**.

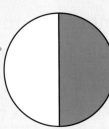

1 of the parts is shaded.

1 out of 2 parts is shaded.

We can say:

One-half is shaded.

A half is shaded.

We can write a half like this:

The number of parts we are thinking about. We call this number the **numerator**.

The total number of equal parts a whole has been divided into. We call this number the **denominator**.

$$\frac{1}{2}$$

We call this line the **division bar**.

We can show a half as:

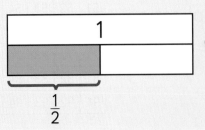

or

As well as finding half of a shape or object, we can find half of a group of objects.

There are 6 cakes on this plate.
Half of them have strawberry icing.
How many cakes have strawberry icing?

> The whole is 6 cakes.

> There are **2 equal groups**.

> The cakes with strawberry icing are half of the whole.

To find half of a group of objects:

1. Count the total number of objects – the whole.

2. **Divide** the whole into 2 equal groups.

3. Count the number of objects in 1 group.

We can show this in a model:

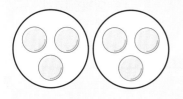 or

6	
○○○	○○○

or

6	
3	3

We can also write this as: $\frac{1}{2}$ of 6 = 3

> 6 divided into 2 equal groups **is equal to** 3 in each group.

Find one-half of the basket of apples.

 Say How would you say this?

 Draw How could you draw this in a model?

 Write How would you write this?

 Is there a link between **dividing by 2** and **halving**?

Pages 56–61

Quarters

Pages 6–7, 46–47, 54–55

To find quarters, we divide the whole into four equal parts. We can find one-quarter, two-quarters or three-quarters of a shape, an object or a group of objects.

Each of these shapes and objects have been **divided into quarters**.

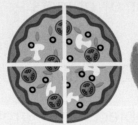  

> Each part is **one-quarter** of the **whole**.

Look at this shape:

> A **quarter** is shaded.

We can say:

> One-quarter is shaded.

> **1 out of 4 parts** is shaded.

We can write one-quarter like this:

> The whole has been divided into equal parts.

1
4

> 1 **part** is shaded.

> There are **4 equal parts**.

Look at this shape:

How is it the same as the circle above? How is it different?

We can say:

> **Two-quarters** are shaded.

> **2 out of 4 parts** are shaded.

We can write two-quarters like this:

> The whole has been divided into equal parts.

2
4

> 2 parts are shaded.

> There are 4 equal parts.

Can you think of another way to describe this shape as a fraction?

56

Look at this shape: How is it the same as the circles on page 56? How is it different? We can say:

Three-quarters are shaded.

3 out of 4 parts are shaded.

We can write three-quarters like this:

The whole has been divided into equal parts.

$\dfrac{3}{4}$

3 parts are shaded.

There are 4 equal parts.

We can show quarters as:

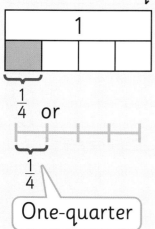

$\dfrac{1}{4}$ or

One-quarter

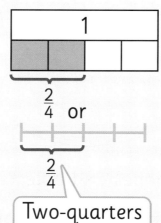

$\dfrac{2}{4}$ or

Two-quarters

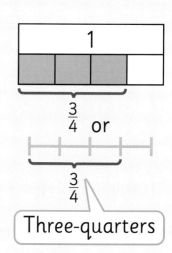

$\dfrac{3}{4}$ or

Three-quarters

To find one-quarter of a group of objects:

1. Count the total number of objects – the whole.

2. **Divide** the whole into 4 equal groups.

3. Count the number of objects in 1 group.

We can show this in a model:

 or

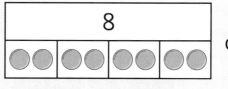 or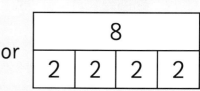

We can also write this as: $\dfrac{1}{4}$ of 8 = 2

8 divided into 4 equal groups is equal to 2 in each group.

How would you find three-quarters of the watermelon pieces?

Pages 58–61

Thirds

Pages 6–7, 46–47, 54–57

A third means one of three equal parts. We can find a third of a shape, an object or a group of objects.

| The whole cake. | The whole cake has been cut into **3 equal parts**. | Each slice of the cake is a **third** of the whole cake. |

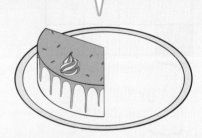

Look at each of these shapes and objects.

Can you spot the shapes and objects that show a third?

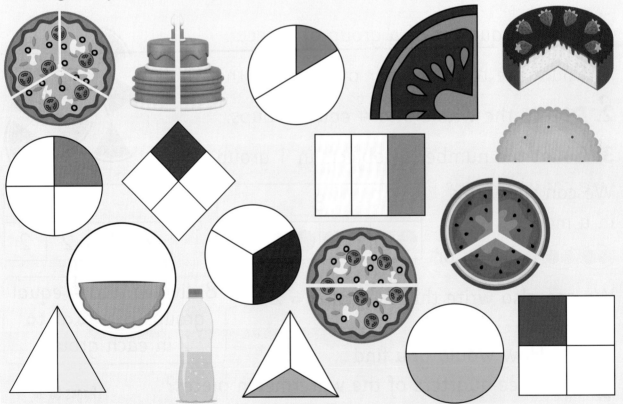

Look at this shape:

The whole has been **divided into** 3 equal parts.

One-third is shaded.

1 of the parts is shaded.

We can say: **1 out of 3 parts** is shaded.

We can write one-third like this:

The whole has been divided into equal parts.

$$\frac{1}{3}$$

1 part is shaded.

There are 3 equal parts.

We can show one-third as:

1		

$\frac{1}{3}$

or

$\frac{1}{3}$

The cars have been divided into **3 equal groups**.

As well as finding one-third of a shape or object, we can find one-third of a group of objects.

To find one-third of a group of objects:

1. Count the total number of objects – the whole.

2. **Divide** the whole into 3 equal groups.

3. Count the number of objects in 1 group.

The whole is 15 cars.

One-third of 15 is 5.

We can show this in a model:

or

15		

or

15		
5	5	5

We can also write this as:
$\frac{1}{3}$ of 15 = 5

15 divided into 3 equal groups **is equal to** 5 in each group.

Pages 60–61

Equivalent fractions and count in fractions

Pages 6–7, 54–59

The same fraction can be described in different ways. For example, half a cake is the same as two-quarters of a cake. These related fractions are called equivalent fractions. Just like with whole numbers, we can count on and back in fractions.

This model is called a fraction wall. It helps show **equivalent fractions** – that is fractions that have the **same value**, or **equal value**.

1				whole
$\frac{1}{2}$		$\frac{1}{2}$		halves
$\frac{1}{4}$	$\frac{1}{4}$	$\frac{1}{4}$	$\frac{1}{4}$	quarters

The fraction wall shows:

2 halves are **equal to** 1 whole.

$$\frac{2}{2} = 1$$

4 quarters are equal to 1 whole.

$$\frac{4}{4} = 1$$

1 half is equal to 2 quarters.

$$\frac{1}{2} = \frac{2}{4}$$

We can also show equivalent fractions using number lines.

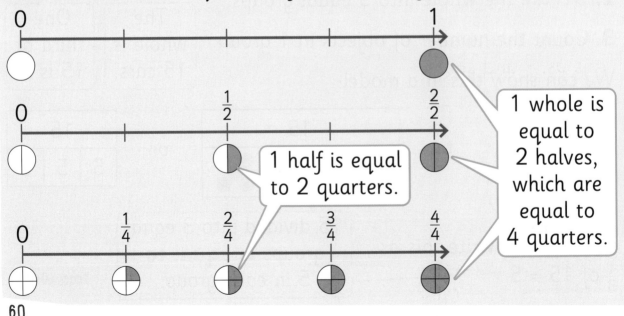

1 half is equal to 2 quarters.

1 whole is equal to 2 halves, which are equal to 4 quarters.

We can use what we know about halves, quarters and **thirds** to **count on** and **count back** in fractions.

Say
- Count on in halves from 0 to 5.
- Count back in halves from 5 to 0.
- Count on and back in halves starting from a number such as $3\frac{1}{2}$.

> We say: **one and a half**.

$$0 \qquad \frac{1}{2} \qquad 1 \qquad 1\frac{1}{2} \qquad 2 \qquad 2\frac{1}{2} \qquad 3 \qquad 3\frac{1}{2} \qquad 4$$

> We can also write this as: $\frac{3}{2}$ and say: **three-halves**.

Say
- Count on in quarters from 0 to 5.
- Count back in quarters from 5 to 0.
- Count on and back in quarters starting from a number such as $3\frac{3}{4}$.

> We say: **one and a quarter**.

$$0 \quad \frac{1}{4} \quad \frac{2}{4} \quad \frac{3}{4} \quad 1 \quad 1\frac{1}{4} \quad 1\frac{2}{4} \quad 1\frac{3}{4} \quad 2 \quad 2\frac{1}{4} \quad 2\frac{2}{4} \quad 2\frac{3}{4} \quad 3$$

> We can also write this as: $\frac{5}{4}$ and say: **five-quarters**.

Use this number line to count on in thirds.

Say
- Count on in thirds from 0 to 5.
- Count back in thirds from 5 to 0.
- Count on and back in thirds starting from a number such as $3\frac{2}{3}$.

$$0 \quad \frac{1}{3} \quad \frac{2}{3} \quad 1 \quad 1\frac{1}{3} \quad 1\frac{2}{3} \quad 2 \quad 2\frac{1}{3} \quad 2\frac{2}{3} \quad 3 \quad 3\frac{1}{3} \quad 3\frac{2}{3} \quad 4$$

Year 2 Number Facts

Addition and subtraction facts to 5, 10 and 20

Addition can be done in any order.

So, 2 + 3 = 5 and
3 + 2 = 5

Addition is the opposite of subtraction.

So, if you know that 3 + 2 = 5 you also know that:
5 − 3 = 2 and 5 − 2 = 3

+	0	1	2	3	4	5	6	7	8	9	10
0	0	1	2	3	4	5	6	7	8	9	10
1	1	2	3	4	5	6	7	8	9	10	11
2	2	3	4	5	6	7	8	9	10	11	12
3	3	4	5	6	7	8	9	10	11	12	13
4	4	5	6	7	8	9	10	11	12	13	14
5	5	6	7	8	9	10	11	12	13	14	15
6	6	7	8	9	10	11	12	13	14	15	16
7	7	8	9	10	11	12	13	14	15	16	17
8	8	9	10	11	12	13	14	15	16	17	18
9	9	10	11	12	13	14	15	16	17	18	19
10	10	11	12	13	14	15	16	17	18	19	20

Multiplication and division facts

2 multiplication table

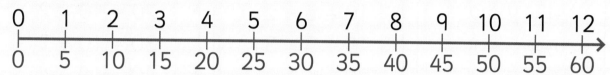

5 multiplication table

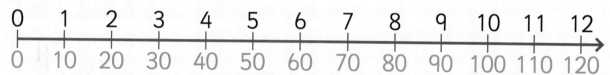

10 multiplication table

2 multiplication table	5 multiplication table	10 multiplication table
1 × 2 = 2	1 × 5 = 5	1 × 10 = 10
2 × 2 = 4	2 × 5 = 10	2 × 10 = 20
3 × 2 = 6	3 × 5 = 15	3 × 10 = 30
4 × 2 = 8	4 × 5 = 20	4 × 10 = 40
5 × 2 = 10	5 × 5 = 25	5 × 10 = 50
6 × 2 = 12	6 × 5 = 30	6 × 10 = 60
7 × 2 = 14	7 × 5 = 35	7 × 10 = 70
8 × 2 = 16	8 × 5 = 40	8 × 10 = 80
9 × 2 = 18	9 × 5 = 45	9 × 10 = 90
10 × 2 = 20	10 × 5 = 50	10 × 10 = 100
11 × 2 = 22	11 × 5 = 55	11 × 10 = 110
12 × 2 = 24	12 × 5 = 60	12 × 10 = 120

Division facts related to the 2 multiplication table

$2 \div 2 = 1$
$4 \div 2 = 2$
$6 \div 2 = 3$
$8 \div 2 = 4$
$10 \div 2 = 5$
$12 \div 2 = 6$
$14 \div 2 = 7$
$16 \div 2 = 8$
$18 \div 2 = 9$
$20 \div 2 = 10$
$22 \div 2 = 11$
$24 \div 2 = 12$

Division facts related to the 5 multiplication table

$5 \div 5 = 1$
$10 \div 5 = 2$
$15 \div 5 = 3$
$20 \div 5 = 4$
$25 \div 5 = 5$
$30 \div 5 = 6$
$35 \div 5 = 7$
$40 \div 5 = 8$
$45 \div 5 = 9$
$50 \div 5 = 10$
$55 \div 5 = 11$
$60 \div 5 = 12$

Division facts related to the 10 multiplication table

$10 \div 10 = 1$
$20 \div 10 = 2$
$30 \div 10 = 3$
$40 \div 10 = 4$
$50 \div 10 = 5$
$60 \div 10 = 6$
$70 \div 10 = 7$
$80 \div 10 = 8$
$90 \div 10 = 9$
$100 \div 10 = 10$
$110 \div 10 = 11$
$120 \div 10 = 12$

1–100 number square

1	2	3	4	5	6	7	8	9	10
11	12	13	14	15	16	17	18	19	20
21	22	23	24	25	26	27	28	29	30
31	32	33	34	35	36	37	38	39	40
41	42	43	44	45	46	47	48	49	50
51	52	53	54	55	56	57	58	59	60
61	62	63	64	65	66	67	68	69	70
71	72	73	74	75	76	77	78	79	80
81	82	83	84	85	86	87	88	89	90
91	92	93	94	95	96	97	98	99	100